EXPLORING MATERIALS
IN MY MAKERSPACE

by Rebecca Sjonger

CRABTREE
PUBLISHING COMPANY
WWW.CRABTREEBOOKS.COM

MATTER AND MATERIALS IN MY MAKERSPACE

Author:
Rebecca Sjonger

Series research and development:
Reagan Miller
Janine Deschenes

Editorial director:
Kathy Middleton

Editor:
Janine Deschenes

Proofreader:
Kelly Spence

Design and photo research:
Katherine Berti

Prepress:
Margaret Amy Salter

Print and production coordinator:
Katherine Berti

Photographs:
All images by Shutterstock

Library and Archives Canada Cataloguing in Publication

Sjonger, Rebecca, author
        Exploring materials in my makerspace / Rebecca Sjonger.

(Matter and materials in my makerspace)
Includes index.
Issued in print and electronic formats.
ISBN 978-0-7787-4607-2 (hardcover).
ISBN 978-0-7787-4623-2 (softcover).
ISBN 978-1-4271-2047-2 (HTML)

        1. Materials--Juvenile literature. 2. Makerspaces--Juvenile literature.
I. Title.

TA418.5.S56 2018   j620.1'12   C2017-907632-9
                                                          C2017-907633-7

Library of Congress Cataloging-in-Publication Data

Names: Sjonger, Rebecca, author.
Title: Exploring materials in my makerspace / Rebecca Sjonger.
Description: New York, New York : Crabtree Publishing Company, [2018] |
    Series: Matter and materials in my makerspace | Includes index.
Identifiers: LCCN 2017057955 (print) | LCCN 2018004615 (ebook) |
    ISBN 9781427120472 (Electronic) |
    ISBN 9780778746072 (hardcover : alk. paper) |
    ISBN 9780778746232 (pbk. : alk. paper)
Subjects: LCSH: Materials--Properties--Juvenile literature. |
    Materials--Experiments--Juvenile literature. |
    Science--Experiments--Juvenile literature. | Makerspaces--Juvenile literature.
Classification: LCC QC173.36 (ebook) | LCC QC173.36 .S5647 2018 (print) |
    DDC 620.1/1--dc23
LC record available at https://lccn.loc.gov/2017057955

Crabtree Publishing Company

www.crabtreebooks.com   1-800-387-7650

Printed in the U.S.A./032018/BG20180202

Published in Canada
Crabtree Publishing
616 Welland Ave.
St. Catharines, Ontario
L2M 5V6

Published in the United States
Crabtree Publishing
PMB 59051
350 Fifth Avenue, 59th Floor
New York, New York 10118

Published in the United Kingdom
Crabtree Publishing
Maritime House
Basin Road North, Hove
BN41 1WR

Published in Australia
Crabtree Publishing
3 Charles Street
Coburg North
VIC 3058

CONTENTS

YOU CAN BE A MAKER!

Makers explore ways to use materials. They use their hands and minds to learn and create new things. Are you ready to dive into your own maker projects? This book will get you started!

TEAM UP

Makers team up to share skills and supplies. They also share their ideas. Makers can teach each other! **Makerspaces** are places where makers work together. Check to see if your community has one. If not, gather some friends to set up your own makerspace!

No right or wrong!

There is no right or wrong way to create something. Makers know that:

- One of the most important tools is a great imagination.
- Each team member adds value to a challenge.
- No ideas are too silly. They could lead to something great!

Makers know that they can learn from each other. Your team members are your most important resource!

MATTER AND MATERIALS

All the materials in this book—and in the world—are made of matter. **Matter is anything that takes up space and has mass. Mass is the amount of material in matter.** We can find these materials in nature or we can make them ourselves.

SOLIDS AND LIQUIDS

One way to describe materials is by their **state**. These are the different forms that matter can take. Two of the main states of matter are **solids** and **liquids**. Solids keep their shape. They cannot be poured. Liquids can be poured. They flow into the shape of whatever holds them.

solids

solid

liquid

liquid

liquids

solid

EXPLORE PROPERTIES

The state of matter is just one of its **properties**. These are the ways we describe materials, such as size or color. Properties help makers sort and choose which supplies to use.

Try it!

Your first challenge is to learn how to explore the properties of materials. Get started on the next page!

PROPERTY DETECTIVE

Many properties can be explored with your senses of sight, touch, smell, taste, and hearing. Ask yourself questions as you explore materials with your senses. What does it feel like when you touch it? What does it look like? Could you taste, listen to, or smell it? Other properties are measured. You could do this with a ruler or a scale.

A ruler is a handy tool to measure the height and length of an object.

Ask an adult for permission before you taste or smell any materials, because some can be dangerous.

PROPERTY CHALLENGE

Some of the materials you may use as a maker are shown below.
Explore some of these common properties to help you get started!

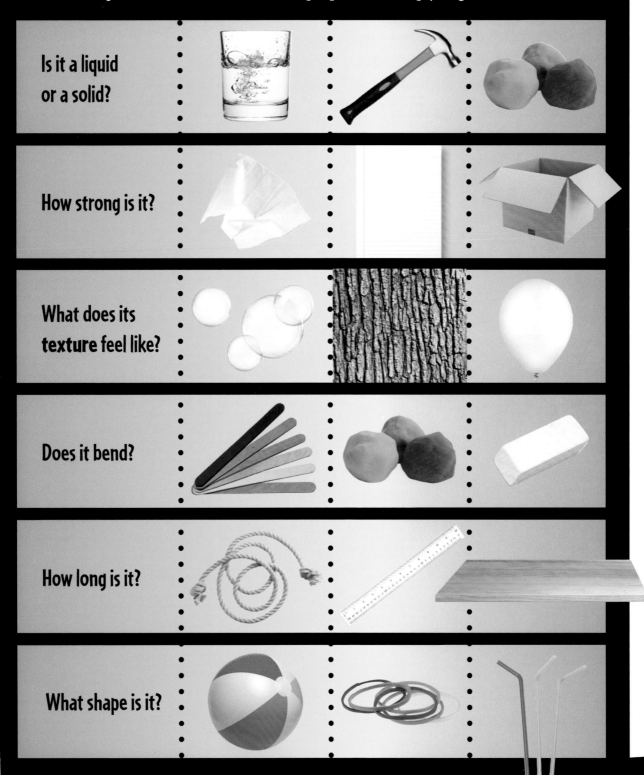

Is it a liquid or a solid?

How strong is it?

What does its texture feel like?

Does it bend?

How long is it?

What shape is it?

HIDDEN PROPERTIES

Not all properties are easy to sense, or explore using your senses. You must be creative with different methods and tools as you explore some materials. Work with other makers to get ideas. Share what you discover!

MAGNETIC MYSTERY

Your senses can tell you a lot about an object. But could they tell if it attracts magnets? No, you will need to experiment with a magnet. See what happens when you place it on a material. Find out about this property on page 26.

Have you made an object using clay? What can your senses tell you about this material?

SOLIDS AND LIQUIDS

Remember, the state of matter is a property. Did you know that some materials can be both solids and liquids? Their states change as they are heated or cooled. This is another property that we cannot sense. It is a fun one to explore!

Ice cream is a solid that becomes a liquid when it heats up.

TEMPERATURE TRICKS

Heating some solids creates liquids. Cooling some liquids makes them solid again! Try melting ice cubes and freezing the water again to see this for yourself. You can also heat some liquids to make solids. For example, what happens when you cook an egg?

MAKER TIPS

Always brainstorm **at the start of a project. By yourself or with a team, think of as many ideas as possible in five minutes. If you work with other makers, respect each person's ideas. Then choose one idea to try!**

PLAN AHEAD

Before you start the mission, plan what you will do. Carefully measure and draw each part. Along the way, be open to changes and new ideas! Where you start may not be where you end up.

When you work with other makers, make sure that you respect each person's ideas.

Help along the way

All makers run into problems during projects. If you run into a problem during a Maker Mission in this book, stick with it and try:

- Making sure each person on your team understands the goal.

- Asking other makers for help. They could help you see the mission in a new way.

- Imagining how you could use the same materials in new ways. Or, think about using different materials.

Material	Properties
paper	solid, white, easy to tear, light
Styrofoam	solid, white, hard to tear, lightest
cardboard	solid, brown, hard to tear, heavy

A t-chart can help you remember the properties you discover. Try it out! Then present your chart to another maker.

HOW HARD IS IT?

Hardness is a common property of materials. Your sense of touch will help you explore it. Have you ever squeezed a fruit to see if it is ripe? If so, you have tested this property! You probably didn't eat the fruit if you decided that it was too hard.

PROPERTY CHECK

Gather at least five kinds of balls. Explore properties such as size or color by looking at the balls. Next, rap them with your knuckles. Squeeze them with your fingers. Rank the balls from most to least hard.

HARD MATERIALS

The hardest balls were made of strong, hard materials. That means they do not break easily. Being fully filled with air also makes a ball hard. Materials that are hard are tougher to cut than soft ones.

Use numbers to rank your balls from most to least hard. List the most hard ball number 1.

Ball	Hardness
bowling ball	1
Ping-Pong ball	3
beach ball	5
football	2
foam ball	4

Bowling balls are very hard because they are used to knock down pins.

Try it!

Put those balls to work in a Maker Mission. Gather some friends to share ideas and supplies. Flip to the next page to get started.

MAKE IT FUN!

MAKER MISSION

Explore how hardness affects how different balls work in bowling. Follow the directions to explore balls found on page 14. Then make your own bowling alley! Mark a spot on the floor and set up pins at least 20 feet (6 m) away. Use at least five different balls to knock them down. Find out whether the hardest ball works best as a bowling ball.

Materials

- Paper
- Pencil
- At least five kinds of balls
- Pins, such as empty plastic bottles
- Measuring tape
- Masking tape, chalk, or ropes

THINK ABOUT IT

Materials

What are the properties of a real bowling ball and pin? Why are they important?

Do other properties, such as the shape, size, texture, or weight of the balls, matter?

Design

Where can you find enough space to set up an alley?

How can you test whether your pins fall over too easily?

Should your test area be on **level** ground?

Does the texture of the ground matter?

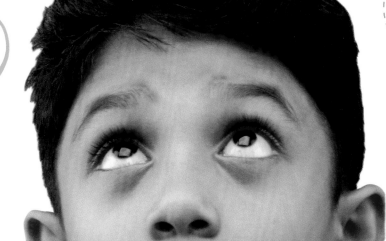

MISSION ACCOMPLISHED

Test your balls in your alley and see what happens. Compare your results with your team. Then, have fun bowling together!

For more project ideas, go to page 30.

CAN YOU SEE THROUGH IT?

One way to sort materials is by how much you can see through them. Matter that you cannot see through is opaque. For example, this book is opaque. Which other opaque objects can you spot around you?

CLEAR AND IN-BETWEEN

You can see all the way through some materials. They are **transparent**, or clear. Other objects are not clear or opaque. They are in-between being completely see-through and completely opaque. The properties of these materials affect how see-through they are. Compare plastic wrap, waxed paper, and cardboard to view this yourself.

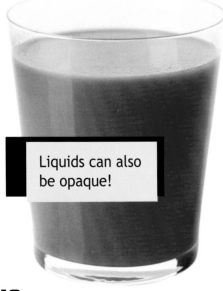

Liquids can also be opaque!

MAKING GLASS

Remember, heating or cooling a material can change its state. Opaque sand can become clear glass! When sand is heated enough, it melts and becomes a hot liquid. This liquid forms glass when it cools. Makers use opaque, clear, and in-between glass. They create things such as stained-glass windows.

Colored glass lets through light. It is in-between clear and opaque.

Try it!

Check out the challenge on the next page to make your own glass-like project. Get started by drawing some ideas.

MAKE A WINDOW

Make a piece of art that looks like a stained-glass window. It must include opaque, clear, and in-between materials.

MAKER MISSION

Materials

- Paper
- Pencil
- Ruler
- Craft supplies, such as construction paper, recycled cardboard, wrapping paper, tissue paper, food packaging, wide tape
- Scissors
- Glue, tape, stapler
- String

THINK ABOUT IT

Design → **Size** → **Materials** → How will you cut holes out of your frame material?

Which parts make the most sense to be opaque?

What size and shape will the outer frame of your window be?

How will you attach the materials?

What kind of design will you put inside the frame?

Do you want to add a hanger so your artwork can be displayed?

MISSION ACCOMPLISHED

Hold up your creation to a light. Can you see through some parts but not others? If you need help, go back to the Maker Tips on page 12. You can do more with these supplies!

Head to page 30 for ideas.

HOW HEAVY IS IT?

All materials have the property of weight. Most solids are heavier than liquids. Their sizes and shapes may help you guess how much they weigh. But just looking at them will not tell you for sure!

COUNT AND COMPARE

Counting materials is one way to explore how heavy they are. Hold up a colored pencil. You can guess how heavy 10 more colored pencils would be. This will not help you compare it to other materials, though. Do you have any ideas for a tool you could use to compare the weights of different materials?

USE A SCALE

A scale measures weight. Some scales measure one object at a time. Other scales balance two objects to see which is heavier.

Scales that balance objects help you compare the weights of two kinds of materials.

Try it!

Go to the Maker Mission on the next page to make your own balancing scale. Stick with it!

MAKE IT BALANCE

Make a balancing scale that compares the weights of different materials. Find at least three solid materials that are as heavy as 1 cup (250 ml) of water.

MAKER MISSION

Materials

- Paper
- Pencil
- String
- Ruler
- Water
- Scissors
- Clothes hanger
- Tape, binder clips
- Liquid measuring cup
- Two of the same containers that hold at least 1 cup (250 ml) of water, such as plastic cups or pails
- Solids for testing, such as marbles, rice, rocks, or popcorn kernels

THINK ABOUT IT

Size
How does the container size limit what you can test?

How can you be sure that your containers hold 1 cup (250 ml) of water?

Materials
Does the shape of the hanger you use matter?

Design
Where will you place the hanger so that it can balance freely?

How will you attach the containers to the hanger so that they start at the same weight? What do you need to measure?

MISSION ACCOMPLISHED

Did you find three solid materials that are as heavy as 1 cup (250 ml) of water? If not, use your imagination! Test any solid that fits in your container.

Check out Endless Ideas on page 30 to do more with your scale.

DOES IT ATTRACT A MAGNET?

Even metals can change states! They can become solids or liquids. Picture how ice cream hardens in a freezer or melts in the heat. Each kind of metal has points when it hardens or softens, just like ice cream.

METALLIC PROPERTIES

Metals have many properties. For example, you could explore their texture or find out if they bend. These are properties you can see or feel. One property of metal cannot be sensed, though. You read about it on page 10. Some of the materials in metals attract magnets! If a metal attracts a metal, it means that it pulls the metal toward its surface and holds it in place.

Some rocks, such as lodestone, are magnetic.

MAGNETIC MATERIALS

Have you ever put a magnet on a metal and found it did not stick? Metals are made up of many materials. Some do not attract magnets. Metals that do attract magnets have nickel and iron in them. Rocks that contain nickel and iron attract magnets, too!

Do you have a magnetic board in your classroom? These boards are made of steel, which is a material made from iron.

Try it!

Flip the page for your next Maker Mission. Start by brainstorming ideas for your own metal sorter.

MAKE A METAL SORTER

Make your own metal sorter to explore magnetic materials. Use a magnet to help you find two metals that are attracted to it and two that are not.

Materials

- Paper
- Pencil
- Handle, such as a wooden ruler
- Large magnet
- Glue, tape, string
- Metals found around your home or school

MAKE IT SAFE

Never put a magnet in your mouth! Magnets can hurt you if you swallow them.

THINK ABOUT IT

Materials

How could you test the strength of your magnet?

Where could you find a variety of metals? Does your home or school have a bin for recycling?

Size

Do you think the size or shape of the magnet you use matters?

Design

How will you attach the magnet to a handle?

Would a long or short handle be better?

MISSION ACCOMPLISHED

Did your sorter find two examples each of metals that attract and do not attract magnets? If not, could you try a different kind of magnet?

Look at Endless Ideas on the next page when you are ready for a new challenge.

ENDLESS IDEAS

Makers are always coming up with something new! Keep exploring materials with these ideas:

Make it fun

pages 16–17

- Work with a friend to get more materials and test as many balls as possible.
- What sort of game could you make with the softest ball? How about with a really big ball?

Make a window

pages 20–21

- Could you use the same materials to make a different design?
- What would happen if the frame was another shape?

Make it balance

pages 24–25

- Invite your friends to guess which of the materials you tested is heavier. Then reveal that they are the same weight!
- Do you think all liquids are the same weight? Test your scale to find out!

Make a metal sorter

pages 28–29

- Use magnets and metals to make a fun game! How could you make a fishing-style game to play with your friends?

LEARNING MORE

BOOKS

Claybourne, Anna. *Experiments with Materials.* Windmill, 2017.

Derosa, Tom, and Carolyn Reeves. *Matter: Its Properties and Its Changes.* New Leaf, 2012.

Oxlade, Chris. *Matter and Materials Experiments.* Powerkids Press, 2016.

Rompella, Natalie. *Experiments in Material and Matter with Toys and Everyday Stuff.* Raintree, 2016.

• •

WEBSITES

Dive into more matter facts:
http://idahoptv.org/sciencetrek/topics/matter/facts.cfm

Try another magnetic maker challenge:
http://pbskids.org/designsquad/build/inspector-detector

Get inspired by the stained-glass-style crafts made by kids:
www.pbs.org/parents/crafts-for-kids/tissue-paper-stained-glass

• •

GLOSSARY

brainstorm To list many ideas—no matter how silly—as quickly as possible

level Flat, without any slope

liquid Matter that can be poured and takes on the shape of its container

makerspace A place where makers work together and share their supplies and skills

mass The measurable amount of material in matter

material Any substance that makes up matter

matter Any material that takes up space and has mass

opaque Describes matter that is not see-through

property A characteristic that describes matter

scale A tool that measures an object's weight, or how heavy it is

solid Matter that does not flow and cannot be poured

state The form that matter takes, such as a solid or a liquid

texture The look or feel of an object, such as soft or rough

transparent Describes matter that is clear and see-through

INDEX

ABOUT THE AUTHOR

Rebecca Sjonger is the author of more than 50 children's books. She has written numerous titles for the *Be a Maker!* and the *Simple Machines in My Makerspace* series.

32